I ♥ COLOURING

Buster Books

With additional material adapted
from www.shutterstock.com

First published in Great Britain in 2015
by Buster Books, an imprint of
Michael O'Mara Books Limited,
9 Lion Yard, Tremadoc Road, London SW4 7NQ

W www.busterbooks.co.uk

f Buster Children's Books

@BusterBooks

ISBN: 978-1-78055-317-7

6 8 10 9 7

This book was printed in September 2015 by L.E.G.O.,
Viale dell'Industria 2, 36100, Vicenza, Italy.

Illustrated by
Felicity French

Edited by
Lauren Farnsworth

Designed by Zoe Bradley
and John Bigwood

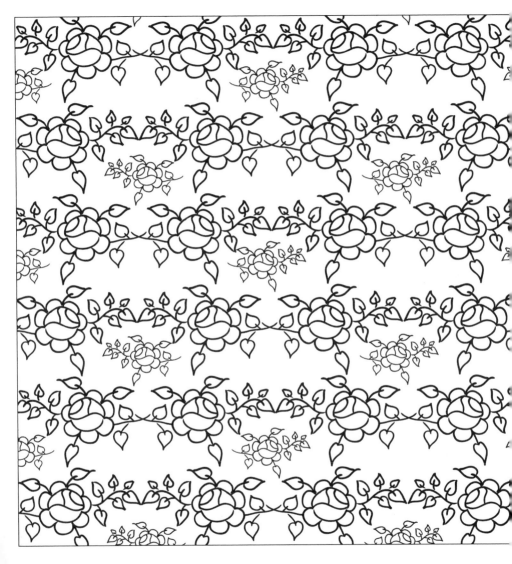

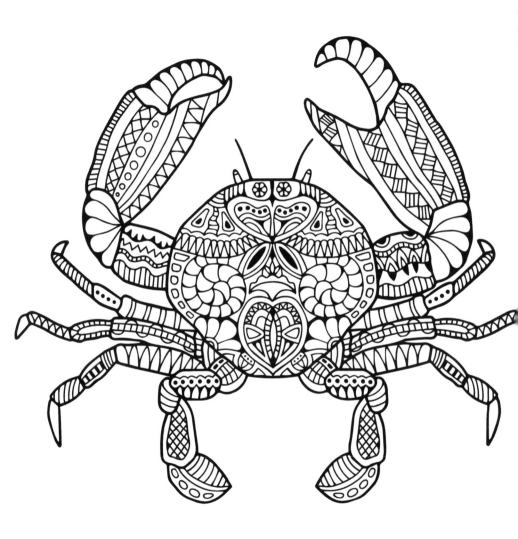